Books

by Judy A. Winter

Consulting Editor: Gail Saunders-Smith, PhD

CAPSTONE PRESS
a capstone imprint

Pebble Books are published by Capstone Press,
151 Good Counsel Drive, P.O. Box 669, Mankato, Minnesota 56002.
www.capstonepub.com

Library of Congress Cataloging-in-Publication Data
Winter, Judy A., 1952–
Jokes about food / by Judy A. Winter.
    p. cm. — (Pebble books. Joke books)
Includes bibliographical references.
Summary: "Simple text and photographs present jokes about food"—Provided by
publisher.
ISBN 978-1-4296-4469-3 (library binding)
1. Food—Juvenile humor. I. Title. II. Series.
PN6231.F66W56 2011
818'.602—dc22   2010002324

Editorial Credits
Gillia Olson, editor; Ted Williams, designer; Sarah Schuette, studio specialist;
Marcy Morin, studio scheduler; Eric Manske, production specialist

Photo Credits
All photos by Capstone Studio: Karon Dubke except: Shutterstock: ID1974, 6,
(background), trucic, background (throughout)

Note to Parents and Teachers

The Joke Books set supports English language arts standards related
to reading a wide range of print for personal fulfillment. Early readers
may need assistance to read some of the words and to use the Table of
Contents, Read More, and Internet Sites sections of this book.

Table of Contents

4

Eggs, Fish, and Bacon Too

How did the egg get off the bus?

It used the eggs-it.

What do you get when you cross a pig and a centipede?

Bacon and legs.

Why did the hamburger join the track team?

Because it's fast food.

What happens to a hamburger that misses school?

It has to ketchup.

What do sea monsters eat for dinner?

Fish and ships.

What did the sardine call the submarine?

A can of people.

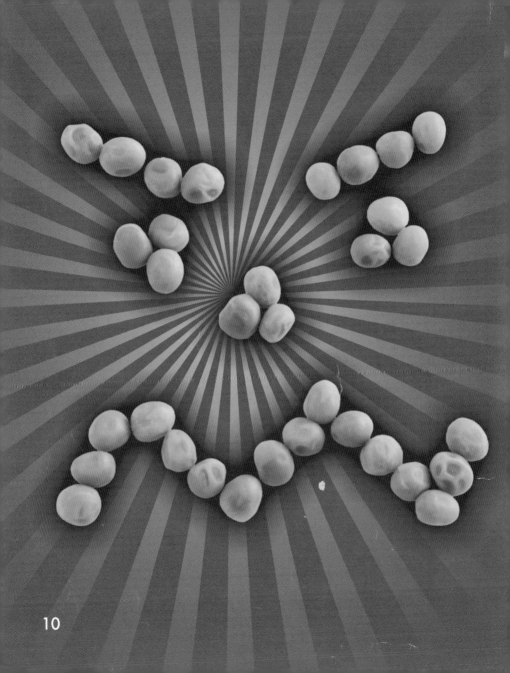

10

What do you call a
pea in a bad mood?

Grump-pea.

Why did the man put
veggies all over the world?

He wanted peas on earth.

What is the difference between broccoli and a booger?

Kids won't eat broccoli.

What is the strongest vegetable?

A muscles sprout.

What do you call two banana peels?

A pair of slippers.

Why did the banana go to the doctor?

It wasn't peeling well.

Why do potatoes make good detectives?

Because they keep their eyes peeled.

What country was the first to fry potatoes?

Greece.

What do firefighters put in their soup?
Firecrackers.

What kind of soup never gets hot?
Chili.

What food talks a lot?

A talk-o.

What kind of food is always cold?

A burrr-ito.

What is a frog's favorite drink?

Croak-a-cola.

How do you make a milk shake?

Scare it.

Read More

Dahl, Michael. *Chewy Chuckles: Deliciously Funny Jokes about Food*. Laugh-It! Readers. Minneapolis: Picture Window, 2003.

Rosenbloom, Joseph. *The Hans Wilhelm Treasury of Jokes*. New York: Sterling, 2009.

Ziegler, Mark. *Lunchbox Laughs: A Book of Food Jokes*. Read-It! Joke Books — Supercharged. Minneapolis: Picture Window, 2005.

Internet Sites

FactHound offers a safe, fun way to find Internet sites related to this book. All of the sites on FactHound have been researched by our staff.

Here's all you do:

Visit *www.facthound.com*

Type in this code: 9781429644693

Word Count: 191   Grade: 1
Early-Intervention Level: 18